SNAKES ALIVE

Sidewinders

by Colleen Sexton

BELLWETHER MEDIA • MINNEAPOLIS, MN

Note to Librarians, Teachers, and Parents:

Blastoff! Readers are carefully developed by literacy experts and combine standards-based content with developmentally appropriate text.

Level 1 provides the most support through repetition of high-frequency words, light text, predictable sentence patterns, and strong visual support.

Level 2 offers early readers a bit more challenge through varied simple sentences, increased text load, and less repetition of high-frequency words.

Level 3 advances early-fluent readers toward fluency through increased text and concept load, less reliance on visuals, longer sentences, and more literary language.

Level 4 builds reading stamina by providing more text per page, increased use of punctuation, greater variation in sentence patterns, and increasingly challenging vocabulary.

Level 5 encourages children to move from "learning to read" to "reading to learn" by providing even more text, varied writing styles, and less familiar topics.

Whichever book is right for your reader, Blastoff! Readers are the perfect books to build confidence and encourage a love of reading that will last a lifetime!

This edition first published in 2011 by Bellwether Media, Inc.

Library of Congress Cataloging-in-Publication Data

Sexton, Colleen A., 1967-
Sidewinders / by Colleen Sexton.
p. cm. – (Blastoff! readers: Snakes alive)
Includes bibliographical references and index.
Summary: "Simple text and full-color photography introduce beginning readers to sidewinders. Developed by literacy experts for students in kindergarten through third grade"–Provided by publisher.
ISBN 978-1-60014-456-1 (hardcover : alk. paper)
1. Crotalus–Juvenile literature. I. Title.
QL666.O69S4925 2010
597.96'38–dc22 2010000711

Printed in the United States of America, North Mankato, MN.

080110 1162

Contents

Sidewinders are small, **venomous** snakes that live in deserts. They are a type of **rattlesnake**.

Sidewinders have triangle-shaped heads and narrow necks. Their flat, thick bodies end in tails that have small **rattles**.

Sidewinders are short snakes. They grow to be about 17 to 30 inches (43 to 76 centimeters) long.

Sidewinders are the color of the sand where they live. They can be brown, yellow, or gray.

Small, square-shaped markings run down their backs. Dark and light bands circle their tails.

Sidewinders have dry, rough **scales** that cover and protect their bodies.

Scales above their eyes look like small horns. These scales protect their eyes from the desert sand.

Sidewinders are found in the southwestern United States and northern Mexico. They live among **dunes** of windblown sand.

Sidewinders get their name from the way they move. A sidewinder throws its head to the side and pulls the rest of its body along.

Sidewinders leave trails of J-shaped tracks in the sand.

Sidewinders travel mostly at night. They stay out of the hot sun during the day.

Sidewinders slide under rocks or bury themselves in the sand to hide. They come out at night to hunt.

Sidewinders stick out their forked tongues to smell the air. They try to pick up the scent of rodents, birds, lizards, and other **prey**.

Sidewinders have two **pits** on their heads that sense heat. The pits allow them to find prey with a **body temperature** warmer than the air.

Sometimes sidewinders toss sand over their bodies. They poke their heads above the sand and wait for prey to come near.

Then they **strike**!
They bite their
prey with sharp,
hollow **fangs**.

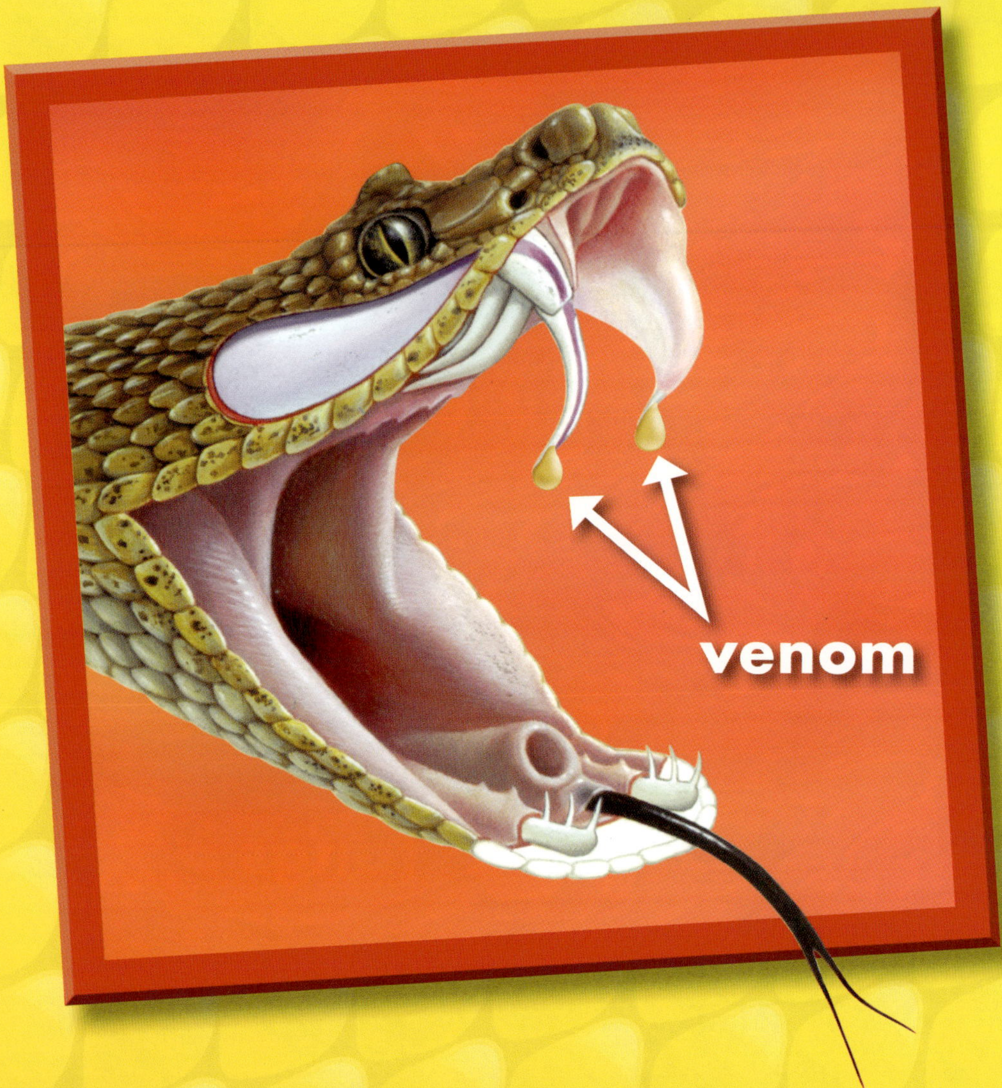

A poison called **venom** flows through the fangs and into the bite. Sidewinders then let go of their prey. The venom soon makes the prey stop breathing.

Sidewinders follow their prey until it stops moving. Then they open their jaws wide and swallow the prey whole!

Glossary

body temperature—the amount of heat in an animal's body; a snake has a body temperature that is the same as its surroundings.

dunes—hills of sand formed by the wind; dunes are most often found in deserts.

fangs—sharp, curved teeth; sidewinders have hollow fangs through which venom can move into a bite.

pits—areas of a snake's face that sense the body heat of an animal; pits tell a snake where an animal is and how big it is.

prey—animals that are hunted by other animals for food

rattles—hard pieces at the end of a rattlesnake's tail that fit together loosely; rattles make buzzing sounds when sidewinders shake their tails.

rattlesnake—a poisonous snake that has heat-sensing pits and a rattle on its tail; rattlesnakes shake their tails as a warning that they will bite.

scales—small plates of skin that cover and protect a snake's body

strike—to quickly throw the head and front part of the body at a predator or prey

venom—a poison that some snakes make; sidewinders have weak venom that is only strong enough to kill small animals.

venomous—able to kill or harm with a poison; the venom that a sidewinder makes is a poison.

To Learn More

AT THE LIBRARY

Gibbons, Gail. *Snakes*. New York, N.Y.: Holiday House, 2007.

Gunzi, Christiane. *The Best Book of Snakes*. New York, N.Y.: Kingfisher, 2003.

Sexton, Colleen. *Rattlesnakes*. Minneapolis, Minn.: Bellwether Media, 2010.

ON THE WEB

Learning more about sidewinders is as easy as 1, 2, 3.

1. Go to www.factsurfer.com.
2. Enter "sidewinders" into the search box.
3. Click the "Surf" button and you will see a list of related Web sites.

With factsurfer.com, finding more information is just a click away.

Index

The images in this book are reproduced through the courtesy of: Jack Goldfarb, front cover, pp. 7, 17; Casey K. Bishop, p. 4 (small); Jack Milchanowski/Photolibrary, pp. 4-5; Rick & Nora Bowers/Alamy, p. 6; R. Andrew Odum/Photolibrary, pp. 8-9; John Cancalosi/Alamy, pp. 10-11; Jon Eppard, pp. 11 (small), 16; Jerry Young/Getty Images, p. 12; Yvette Cardozo/Photolibrary, p. 13; Patricio Robles Gil/Photolibrary, p. 14 (small); Karl Terblanche/Ardea, pp. 14-15; Rex Lisman/Getty Images, pp. 18-19; Tom McHugh/Photo Researchers, Inc., p. 19 (small); National Geographic/Getty Images, p. 20; Kevin P., p. 21.